FAST!
BULLET TRAINS
... and other fast machines on rails

QEB Publishing

IAN GRAHAM

The words in **bold** are explained in the Glossary on page 30.

Front cover: This Chinese train is one of the many high-speed trains developed after the first bullet trains in Japan (see page 16).

Project Editor: Angela Royston
Designer: Andrew Crowson
Picture Researcher: Maria Joannou

Copyright © QEB Publishing, Inc. 2010

Published in the United States by
QEB Publishing, Inc.
3 Wrigley, Suite A
Irvine, CA 92618

www.qed-publishing.co.uk

Library of Congress Cataloging-in-Publication Data

Graham, Ian, 1953-
  Bullet trains / Ian Graham.
    p. cm. -- (Fast!)
  Includes bibliographical references and index.
  ISBN 978-1-59566-927-8 (library binding : alk. paper)
  1. High speed trains--Juvenile literature. I. Title.
  TF1455.G73 2011
  385'.22--dc22
                    2010006060

Printed in China

Picture credits
Alamy Images R A Rayworth 9tl, Trinity Mirror/Mirrorpix 12–13, Jack Sullivan 13tl, Clynt Garnham Transportation 18; **Cedar Point Amusement Park** 14; **Corbis** 26–27, Hulton-Deutsch Collection 5tl & b, Bettmann 10–11, 11tr, Paul Almasy 17bl, Steve Kaufman 17br, Michel Ginfray/Sygma 20–21, G. Bowater 22–23, Paul Souders 25t; **Getty Images** STR/Stringer FC, Science & Society Picture Library 6t, 6–7, 7c, 13tr, AFP/Stan Honda 15t, AFP/Yoshokazu Tsuno 17t, Superstock 20b, 21bl, Koichi Kamoshida/Stringer 25br, Ralph Crane/Time Life Pictures 26t; **National Railway Museum** SSPL 9tr; **Photolibrary** Paul Nevin 2, 8–9, Photononstop/Alain Marcay 5tr, 22t, Imagestate/Gordan Nicholson 12t, Japan Travel Bureau 16, Picture Press/Harald Schoen 19tl, SGM SGM 23tl, Imagebroker.net/Marijan Murat 23tr; **Photoshot** UPPA/Andrew_Gombert 15b, ChinaFotoPress 24t; **Rex Features** 21br; **Shutterstock** Holger Mette 24–25, John Leung BC; **Siemens** 19tr; **Talgo (Deutschland) GmbH** 11tl; **Topham Picturepoint** The Granger Collection 7t, 8t; **U.S. Air Force** 27t; **Wikimedia Commons** HMSO/Crown Copyright 4t & b, Kgrr (cc) 2007 by Konrad Roeder 19b, AllenS 27c. Illustrations on pages 28 and 29 by Leonardo Meschini, based on graphics courtesy of Discovery Communications

Contents

Note: The trains appear in order of speed, from the slowest to the fastest.

Fastest on rails

When the railway age began 200 years ago, it was quicker to go by horse than to catch a train. Soon, trains overtook horses and the railway became the fastest way to travel.

The first steam train

In 1804, Richard Trevithick built the world's first successful **locomotive** powered by steam. Trevithick's locomotive pulled coal wagons at the Penydarren ironworks in Wales, but it wasn't fast. It took four hours to haul 10 tons of coal 10 miles (16 kilometers), but it proved that locomotives could pull heavy loads.

The Penydarren locomotive ran on thin, flat iron rails.

The large wheel on Richard Trevithick's Penydarren locomotive helped the engine to run smoothly.

Locomotion

- Type: Steam
- Country: United Kingdom
- Top speed: 15 miles per hour (24 kilometers per hour)

HOW FAST?

Locomotion went about five times faster than a person walking.

High-speed trains provide fast inter-city travel.

Going faster

In 1825, George and Robert Stephenson built a locomotive called *Locomotion*. It too carried coal but was six times faster than Trevithick's locomotive. Today, high-speed trains carry passengers at speeds as fast as racing cars. **Experimental** trains go even faster.

Stephenson's *Locomotion* was in service until 1841.

Rocket

A steam locomotive called *Rocket* was built specially for a competition in 1829. It proved to be the best and the fastest.

Rocket was built specially for the Rainhill Trials.

The Rainhill Trials

While the Liverpool and Manchester Railway was being built in England in the 1820s, a competition was held to find the best locomotive to pull trains on the railway. Five locomotives took part in the competition, which was called the Rainhill Trials. Thousands of people lined the tracks to see the trains.

ROCKET.

A clear winner

The Trials went on for eight days. Most of the locomotives broke down, but *Rocket* kept going and was the clear winner. It was built by George Stephenson and his son Robert. *Rocket* reached a top speed of 30 miles per hour (48 kilometers per hour), and managed to haul a load weighing more than 13 tons.

George Stephenson prepares *Rocket* for its run in the Rainhill Trials.

This is an exact copy of *Rocket*. It was built to show people what the first trains were like.

LIVERPOOL TRAVELLER MANCHESTER
RAILWAY — COMPANY

FACTFILE

Rocket

- Type: Steam
- Country: United Kindgom
- Top speed: 30 miles per hour (48 kilometers per hour)

HOW FAST?

Rocket went about as fast as cars are allowed to travel in towns.

Flying Scotsman

Several trains are said to have set speed records in the 1890s and early 1900s, but no one could be sure if the records were correct. To solve this problem, trains started carrying equipment for measuring speed when they tried to break records.

Empire State Express ran between New York City and Buffalo in the 1890s.

Early claims

In 1893, a U.S. locomotive called *Empire State Express No.999* was said to have reached 110 miles per hour (180 kilometers per hour). In 1904, a British locomotive called *City of Truro* was said to have gone faster than 99 miles per hour (160 kilometers per hour). However, these trains did not have speed-recording equipment on board, so no one knows exactly how fast they really went.

Flying Scotsman toured Australia in 1989.

City of Truro steams through Wales.

Official record

On November 30, 1934, a British locomotive called *Flying Scotsman* carried equipment on board to measure its speed. The equipment measured its speed at 99 miles per hour (160 kilometers per hour), the first **official** rail speed record.

Pioneer Zephyr

In the 1930s, railway bosses in the USA were looking for ways to persuade more people to travel by train. The Chicago, Burlington, and Quincy Railroad built a fantastic new train, which was powered by a diesel engine.

Pioneer Zephyr speeds to a world record.

Train from the future

The gleaming silver-colored *Pioneer Zephyr* looked like a train from the future. On May 26, 1934, it made a "dawn-to-dusk dash" from Denver to Chicago. All other trains were cleared out of its way. During the 1015-mile (1633-kilometer) journey, *Pioneer Zephyr* reached a new world record speed of 112 miles per hour (181 kilometers per hour).

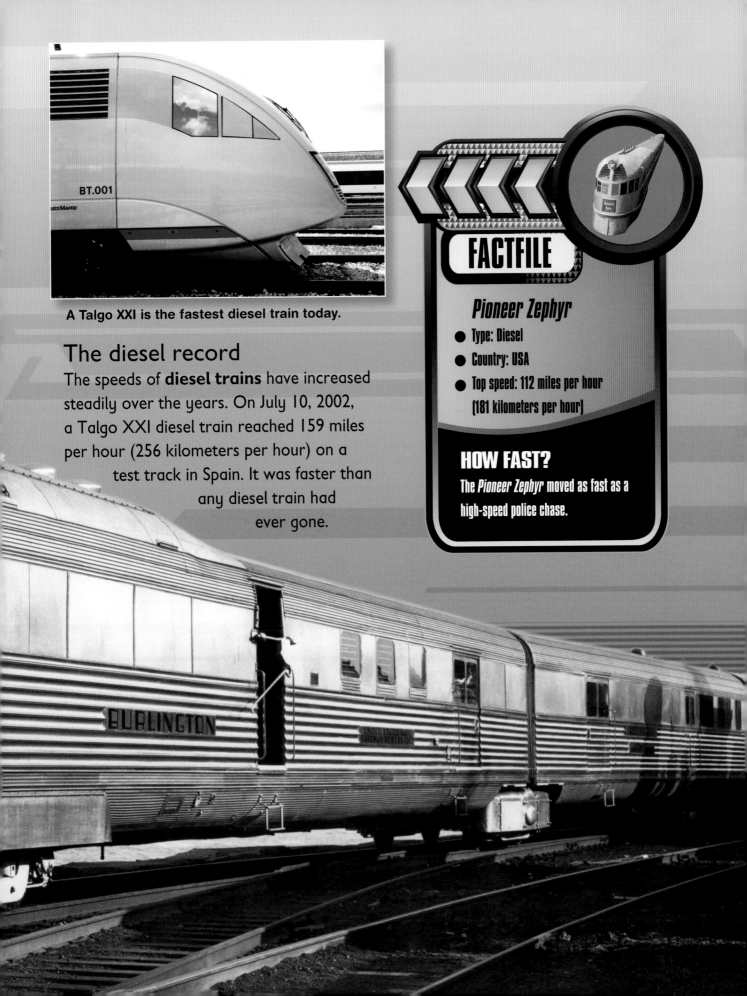

A Talgo XXI is the fastest diesel train today.

The diesel record

The speeds of **diesel trains** have increased steadily over the years. On July 10, 2002, a Talgo XXI diesel train reached 159 miles per hour (256 kilometers per hour) on a test track in Spain. It was faster than any diesel train had ever gone.

FACTFILE

Pioneer Zephyr

● Type: Diesel
● Country: USA
● Top speed: 112 miles per hour (181 kilometers per hour)

HOW FAST?

The *Pioneer Zephyr* moved as fast as a high-speed police chase.

BT.001

Mallard

In the 1930s, more and more people were driving cars, and some were already traveling by air. Railways tried to keep passengers traveling by train by showing how fast and reliable trains were.

Mallard

The London and North Eastern Railway (LNER) company decided to build new, faster trains. The result was a series of **streamlined** steam locomotives called A4s. One of these new locomotives, called *Mallard*, made history.

Mallard was an A4 Pacific Class steam locomotive.

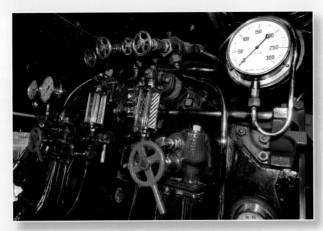
Mallard was controlled by a complicated set of levers and valves.

The last steam record

On July 3, 1938, *Mallard* set off with a team of **engineers** who thought they were doing some ordinary tests. When they were on board, they were told that the train was going to try to break the world rail speed record. Speed-recording equipment had already been loaded onto the train. *Mallard* reached a record-breaking speed of 126 miles per hour (202 kilometers per hour). This is still the world record for a steam train.

FACTFILE

Mallard
- Type: Steam
- Country: United Kingdom
- Top speed: 126 miles per hour (202 kilometers per hour)

HOW FAST?
At top speed, *Mallard* was about twice as fast as a car on a highway.

Mallard's wedge-shaped nose helped it to go faster than any other steam train.

4468   L N E R

Roller coasters

Roller coasters use rail tracks to give an exciting ride. The cars on the most recent roller coasters speed around twists, turns, and loops. Some roller coasters are very fast indeed.

The top thrill

In the 1970s, the fastest roller coasters had a top speed of about 62 miles per hour (100 kilometers per hour). New roller coasters went faster and faster. When the *Top Thrill Dragster* roller coaster opened in Ohio, in 2003, it became the world's fastest. Its cars reached a top speed of 118 miles per hour (190 kilometers per hour).

The *Top Thrill Dragster* track snakes up and down a tower as tall as a skyscraper.

14

The fastest ride

Top Thrill Dragster held the record for two years until *Kingda Ka* opened in New Jersey. Its **launch system** boosts the cars to a top speed of 128 miles per hour (206 kilometers per hour) in only 3.5 seconds. The system sends them climbing up a tower 456 feet (139 meters) high—as tall as a 45-floor building. This makes *Kingda Ka* the tallest roller coaster, as well as the fastest.

FACTFILE

Kingda Ka

- Type: Roller coaster
- Country: USA
- Top speed: 128 miles per hour (206 kilometers per hour)

HOW FAST?

Kingda Ka is as fast as a sports car.

Kingda Ka is the tallest and fastest roller coaster.

Bullet trains

The first high-speed electric passenger trains were built in Japan. They quickly became known as "bullet trains," because their nose is shaped like a bullet.

Special tracks

The first bullet trains in the 1960s ran at 130 miles per hour (210 kilometers per hour). They held several world speed records. Today, the latest bullet trains run at about 185 miles per hour (300 kilometers per hour) and even faster trains are being designed. They run on special tracks that are as straight and level as possible. Tight bends and uneven tracks would slow the trains down.

The 500 Series bullet train was introduced in 1997.

High voltage

The trains have up to 14 passenger carriages and can be 1,300 feet (400 meters) long. Their **electric motors** are powered from 25,000-**volt** cables hanging above the track. Earthquakes are common in Japan. If the tracks are shaken by a strong earthquake, the trains stop **automatically** and safely.

Japan's bullet trains run on special high-speed tracks.

Japan's original 0 Series bullet trains ran from 1964 until 2008.

FACTFILE

N700 Shinkansen train

- Type: Electric
- Country: Japan
- Top speed: 185 miles per hour (300 kilometers per hour)

HOW FAST?

The fastest bullet trains are as fast as a racing car at top speed.

High-speed trains

Japan's bullet trains showed the rest of the world the future of passenger rail travel. In the following 30 years, a number of new high-speed electric railways were built in other countries.

High-speed rail

The French TGV came first in 1981. Then Germany built its ICE trains. They have been carrying passengers since 1989. Spain's AVE came next in 1992. Then in 2000, the Acela Express started running between Boston and Washington D.C. It tilts as it goes around bends to make the journey smoother.

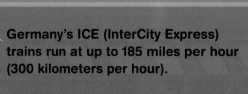

Germany's ICE (InterCity Express) trains run at up to 185 miles per hour (300 kilometers per hour).

AVE Class 103

- Type: Electric
- Country: Spain
- Top speed: 250 miles per hour (403 kilometers per hour)

HOW FAST?

The AVE class 103's record-breaking top speed is more than four times faster than a car on a highway.

Spain's AVE 103 is the world's fastest passenger train.

The Acela Express carries more than 3 million passengers a year.

Spanish record

A Spanish AVE Class 103 train broke the record for the fastest passenger train on July 16, 2006. It reached a speed of 250 miles per hour (403 kilometers per hour) while traveling between Madrid and Zaragoza. Special record-breaking trains have gone faster, but this was an ordinary passenger train.

Air trains

Different train-makers have tried to build trains that glide on a cushion of air. There have been "air train" projects in the USA and France.

Aerotrain

In the 1950s, the U.S. General Motors car company built the Aerotrain. Its diesel locomotive looked like a 1950s motor car. The carriages sat on bags full of air. The air-bags were supposed to give passengers a smoother ride. However, when the trains neared their top speed, the carriages bounced around uncomfortably.

Only two Aerotrains were ever built.

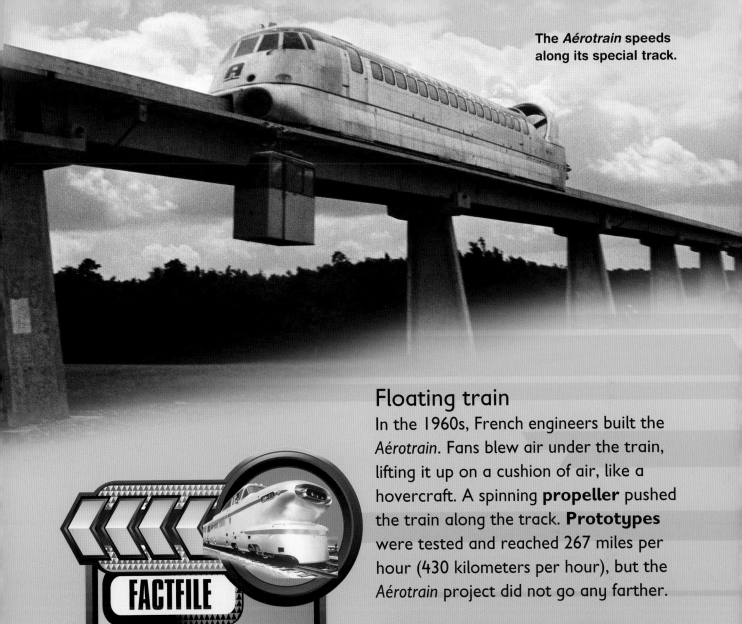

The *Aérotrain* speeds along its special track.

Floating train

In the 1960s, French engineers built the *Aérotrain*. Fans blew air under the train, lifting it up on a cushion of air, like a hovercraft. A spinning **propeller** pushed the train along the track. **Prototypes** were tested and reached 267 miles per hour (430 kilometers per hour), but the *Aérotrain* project did not go any farther.

FACTFILE

Aérotrain

- Type: Hovertrain
- Country: France
- Top speed: 267 miles per hour (430 kilometers per hour)

HOW FAST?

The French *Aérotrain* would easily win a race against any racing car today.

This rocket-powered *Aérotrain* reached a speed of 214 miles per hour (345 kilometers per hour) in 1966.

TGV

The TGV was the first high-speed train built in Europe after Japan's bullet trains. It set a string of speed records.

Radio signals

TGV trains run on high-speed tracks throughout France and in some nearby countries. The trains go so fast that the drivers can't see signals beside the track. Instead, signal information is sent by radio into the driver's cab.

A TGV power car is immensely powerful.

A TGV Atlantique train speeds through the French countryside.

A TGV train is powered by electricity.

Super-TGV

TGVs travel at up to 200 miles per hour (320 kilometers per hour), but one TGV went a lot faster. It was shorter than usual, and the electric cable above the track supplied the train with 31,000 volts instead of the usual 25,000. This train was more than twice as powerful as a normal TGV. On April 3, 2007, it set a record speed for passenger trains of 357 miles per hour (574 kilometers per hour).

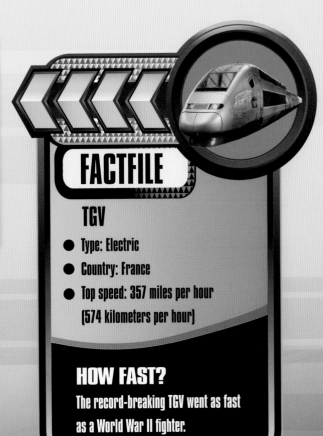

FACTFILE

TGV

- Type: Electric
- Country: France
- Top speed: 357 miles per hour (574 kilometers per hour)

HOW FAST?

The record-breaking TGV went as fast as a World War II fighter.

Flying trains

The fastest trains fly above their track! Without wheels rolling on rails, they can go a lot faster. These trains are called maglevs.

Magnetic trains

A maglev is a magnetic levitation train. The train and its special track are both magnetic. When two magnets are brought close together, they either snap together or push each other apart. Maglevs use the push of this powerful magnetic force to lift a whole train off the ground.

Maglevs run on tracks that are called guideways.

This German high-speed train, called Transrapid, is a maglev.

Chinese maglev

The first passenger-carrying maglev opened for business in Shanghai, China, in 2004. The trains, which were designed in Germany, usually travel at up to 217 miles per hour (350 kilometers per hour) between the city of Shanghai and its international airport. One train reached 311 miles per hour (501 kilometers per hour) in a test run in 2003. Experimental maglevs have gone even faster. In 2003, a Japanese experimental maglev called *MLX01* reached a world record speed of 361 miles per hour (581 kilometers per hour).

The Shanghai maglev approaches a station.

FACTFILE

MLX01

● Type: Maglev
● Country: Japan
● Top speed: 361 miles per hour (581 kilometers per hour)

HOW FAST?
Japan's *MLX01* maglev goes at more than half the speed of a jet airliner.

Rocket sleds

The fastest rail vehicles are rocket sleds. A rocket sled is a vehicle fired along a rail at great speed by rockets.

High-speed tests

Rocket sleds are used to test the shape of high-speed vehicles, such as aircraft, **missiles**, and cars that set land speed records. A **model** of the vehicle, or just its nose, is bolted to the sled and fired down the rail. Cameras beside the track show what happens to the model.

Technicians prepare a rocket sled for a test firing.

Part of a missile is boosted to a high speed by a rocket sled during a test.

In the 1950s, people rode on rocket sleds to test the effect on their body.

Fastest ever

The highest speed ever reached by a rocket sled is 6,589 miles per hour (10,604 kilometers per hour). It's the world record speed for any rail vehicle, ever. The record was set on January 31, 2008, at the Holloman Air Force Base in New Mexico. The track is called the High-Speed Test Track. It is 50,790 feet (15,480 meters) long and dead straight. It is used to test parachutes, the shape of new rockets, new types of aircraft engines, and **ejection seats**.

FACTFILE

Holloman Air Force Base Test Track

- Type: Rocket sled track
- Country: USA
- Top speed: 6,589 miles per hour (10,604 kilometers per hour)

HOW FAST?

The Holloman rocket sled can travel the length of 32 football fields every second!

27

Future records

Imagine catching a train in London, U.K., and going non-stop to New York in less than an hour! Some engineers think it might be possible to do this!

Atlantic tunnel

The plan is to send ultra-high-speed trains through a railway tunnel that floats just under the surface of the Atlantic Ocean. Cables **anchored** to the ocean floor would hold the tunnel in position. Inside the tunnel, maglev trains would travel at almost 5,000 miles per hour (8,000 kilometers per hour), or nearly ten times faster than a jet airliner.

Cables would hold this futuristic railway tunnel in place under the water.

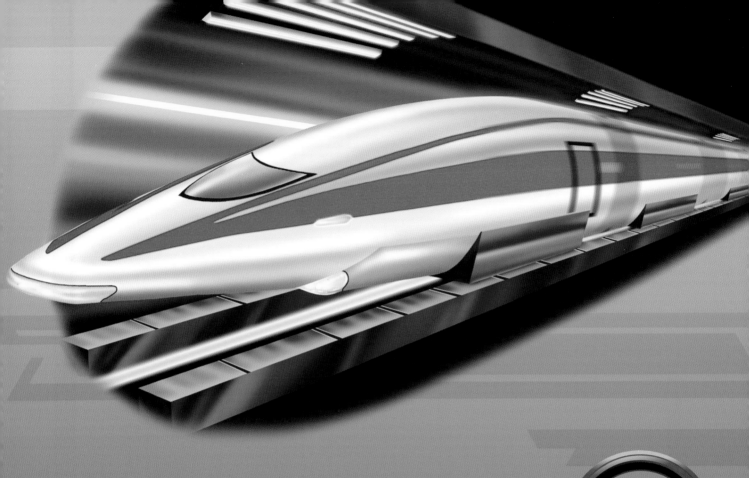

An artist's impression of a maglev train flying through the underwater tunnel.

Airtight train

A train traveling at such a high speed would be slowed down too much by air in the tunnel, so the air would have to be taken out of the tunnel. The train would be sealed, so it would need its own air supply for the people inside to breathe, like a spaceship. No one knows if this amazing project will ever be built.

FACTFILE

Transatlantic train

- **Type:** Maglev
- **Country:** Europe/USA
- **Top speed:** 5,000 miles per hour (8,000 kilometers per hour)

HOW FAST?

The transatlantic maglev would be 20 times faster than a passenger train today.

Glossary

anchored Held firmly in one place.

automatically Working on its own without any need for someone to operate controls.

diesel train A train pulled by a locomotive that is powered by a diesel engine.

ejection seat A rocket-powered seat that fires a pilot out of a military plane in an emergency.

electric motor A machine that changes electricity into movement. Electric trains use electric motors to power their wheels.

engineer Someone who uses scientific and technical knowledge to design and repair machines, including trains.

experimental Built specially to test something new, such as a new shape of train or a new type of engine, or to set a speed record.

launch system The mechanism that starts a roller coaster moving at the start of each run.

locomotive An engine that moves under its own power and pulls trains.

missile A weapon powered by a rocket or jet engine that steers itself toward a target and then explodes.

model A copy of something, usually smaller than the real thing and sometimes built for tests.

official Believed to be true by an important organization.

propeller A device with angled blades that spins and pushes a vehicle along.

prototype The first example of something to be built.

streamlined With a shape that moves through the air as easily as possible, causing the least resistance to the air flowing around it.

volt A unit of voltage or electric force.

Notes for parents and teachers

Shape and size

Look through the pictures in the book and talk about the trains they show and why they are different shapes and sizes. Are they like other trains you have seen or traveled on, or are they different?

Controls

Talk about how a driver controls a train, by using a lever to go faster and brakes to slow down. Does a train have a steering wheel like a car? Does it need one?

Electric power

The fastest trains are powered by electricity. Diesel engines are big and heavy, and need big tanks of diesel oil to burn in the engine. Talk about why the fastest trains don't have these big heavy engines. Hint: can you run faster when you're carrying a big, heavy load? Why do you think flying trains (maglevs) can go faster than trains with big steel wheels rolling on steel rails?

Tracks

Talk about why the fastest passenger trains run on their own specially laid tracks. Why don't they use the same bumpy, windy tracks as other trains?

Fun on rails

Roller coasters are probably the most fun of any vehicle on rails. Do you think more people would travel by train if trains looped, twisted, and turned upside down like roller coasters?

Future trains

If the train tunnel under the Atlantic Ocean is ever built, would you like to travel through it? What would it be like to go by train through an underwater tunnel nearly ten times faster than an airliner?

Drawing

Ask children to draw their own record-breaking train. What would it look like? What shape would it be? What sort of engine would it have? Would it be electric, or would it have a jet engine? How fast do they think it would go?

Index